BIRDS

Birds

Birds

With a seemingly endless range of shapes, sizes and forms, birds have fascinated people for as long as anyone can remember. Their bright plumage, incredible antics and melodious songs bring joy and life to virtually every habitat on Earth.

These remarkable creatures have inspired artists and writers alike for many centuries, even millennia, and this book is intended as a celebration of the relationship between birds and people. Stunning watercolour paintings

and other artworks are coupled with quotes about birds – some very well known and others less famous.

So prepare for a journey around the world – from the Americas to Australia, and from Asia to Antarctica – exploring many aspects that we love about our feathered friends.

"When a cardinal
appears in your yard,
it's a visitor from heaven."

– OLD FOLKLORE SAYING

"Owl is the grand and rather clever old man of the forest. He can also spell Tuesday."

– A. A. MILNE

"*Quick as a hummingbird,
she darts so eagerly,
swiftly, sweetly
– dipping into the
flowers of my heart.*"

– JAMES OPPENHEIM

"A woodpecker can tap twenty times on a thousand trees and get nowhere, but stay busy. Or he can tap twenty-thousand times on one tree and get dinner."

– SETH GODIN

"The moment a little boy
is concerned with which is a
jay and which is a sparrow,
he can no longer see the birds
or hear them sing."

— ERIC BERNE

"True hope is swift,
and flies with
swallow's wings."

– WILLIAM SHAKESPEARE

"It's practically impossible to look at a penguin and feel angry."

– JOEL MOORE

"Always be on the lookout
for the presence of wonder."

– E. B. WHITE

"*Wherever you go,
no matter what the weather,
always bring your own
sunshine.*"

– ANTHONY J. D'ANGELO

"And a good south wind
sprung up behind;
The Albatross did follow,
And every day,
for food or play,
Came to the mariner's hollo!"

– SAMUEL TAYLOR COLERIDGE

"A magpie can be happy or sad: sometimes so happy that he sits on a high, high gum tree and rolls the sunrise around in his throat like beads of pink sunlight; and sometimes so sad that you would expect the tears to drip off his beak."

– COLIN THIELE

*"The gull sees farthest
who flies highest."*

– RICHARD BACH

"Magic birds were dancing in the mystic marsh. The grass swayed with them, and the shallow waters, and the earth fluttered under them. The earth was dancing with the cranes, and the low sun, and the wind and sky."

— MARJORIE KINNAN RAWLINGS

"When I see a rainbow,
I know that someone,
somewhere loves me."

– ANTHONY T. HINCKS

"*Neither the hummingbird nor the flower wonders how beautiful it is.*"

– UNKNOWN

"There are no ugly ducklings."

– LORETTA YOUNG

"I'm doubtful about the temper of your flamingo. Shall I try the experiment?"

– LEWIS CARROLL

"Strictly confined to the tropical portions of America, [toucans] are a retiring and shy race, are mostly observed in small flocks or companies, and inhabit the dense woods and forests of that luxuriant country."

– JOHN GOULD

"A thing of beauty
is a joy forever:
its loveliness increases;
it will never pass
into nothingness."

– JOHN KEATS

"*Hummingbird –*
with brave wings she flies."

– UNKNOWN

"She blushed and I smiled
when we saw the Magpie
look at us
while we kissed below
the Acacia tree!"

– AVIJEET DAS

"Relationships are like birds.
If you hold tightly, they die.
If you hold loosely, they fly.
But if you hold with care,
they remain with you forever."

– UNKNOWN

"To me, the garden is
a doorway to other worlds;
one of them, of course,
is the world of birds."

– ANNE RAVER

"It is not only fine feathers that make fine birds."

– AESOP

"Birds are the last of the dinosaurs."

– NEIL GAIMAN

*"Find beauty not only
in the thing itself
but in the pattern
of the shadows,
the light and dark which
that thing provides."*

– JUN'ICHIRŌ TANIZAKI

"For some reason
parrots have to bite me.
That's their job.
I don't know why that is.
They've nearly torn
my nose off.
I've had some really
bad parrot bites."

– STEVE IRWIN

"When robins appear,
loved ones are near."

– UNKNOWN

"There's a fine line between fishing and just standing on the shore like an idiot."

– STEVEN WRIGHT

*"Patience is the
road to wisdom."*

– KAO KALIA YANG

"Blue was never so beautiful blue."

– PETRA HERMANS

"At home, I love reaching out into that absolute silence, when you can hear the owl or the wind."

– AMANDA HARLECH

"*No bird soars too high if he soars with his own wings.*"

– WILLIAM BLAKE

"For one to thrive, the other should always wither. After all, for a woodpecker to live, the tree must always suffer."

– HIRANMAYEE BALAJI

"We should preserve every scrap of biodiversity as priceless while we learn to use it and come to understand what it means to humanity."

– E. O. WILSON

"There is no way to happiness – happiness is the way."

– THICH NHAT HANH

"At once the bush was filled with laughter. Wild kookaburras ... had flown into a nearby tree, and they made a terrible din, chuckling and laughing at the top of their voices. Nobody could speak for the noise."

– DOROTHY WALL

"A heart without dreams
is like a bird
without feathers."

– SUZY KASSEM

"A crown is merely a hat
that lets the rain in."

– FREDERICK THE GREAT

"Never look for birds
of this year in the
nests of the last."

– MIGUEL DE CERVANTES

"*Be a parrot in a flock of pigeons.*"

– UNKNOWN

*"The thankful receiver
bears a plentiful harvest."*

– WILLIAM BLAKE

"*In order to see birds,
it is necessary to become
a part of the silence.*"

– ROBERT LYND

"Hope is the thing
with feathers,
That perches in the soul,
And sings the tune
without the words,
and never stops at all."

– EMILY DICKINSON

"A wonderful bird
is the pelican.
His bill will hold more
than his belican."

– DIXON LANIER MERRITT

*"Play not the Peacock,
looking everywhere about you,
to see if you be well deck't."*

– GEORGE WASHINGTON

"She was a coquette;
he was sure she had a spirit
of her own; but in her bright,
sweet, superficial little visage
there was no mockery,
no irony."

– HENRY JAMES

"You can observe a lot
by just watching."

– YOGI BERRA

"*There is no blue without yellow and without orange.*"

– VINCENT VAN GOGH

"*What bird has the most elaborate, the most complex, and the most beautiful song in the world? I guess there are lots of contenders but this bird must be one of them. The Superb Lyrebird.*"

– DAVID ATTENBOROUGH

"The eyes like sentinel
occupy the highest place
in the body."

– MARCUS TULLIUS CICERO

"You cannot fly like an eagle with the wings of a wren."

– WILLIAM HENRY HUDSON

"*I would like to paint
the way a bird sings.*"

– CLAUDE MONET

"Scientists have reported that elephants grieve their dead, monkeys perceive injustice and cockatoos like to dance to the music of the Backstreet Boys."

– HAL HERZOG

"Look at the sparrows;
they do not know what they
will do in the next moment.
Let us literally live
from moment to moment."

– MAHATMA GANDHI

"An owl is the wisest
of all birds because
the more it sees
the less it talks."

– CHRISTIE WATSON

"An upstart is a sparrow
eager to marry a hornbill."

– PROVERB FROM MALAWI

"If an emu wants one
of your sandwiches,
he will get it,
and then run away.
He cannot help you
with your sudoku."

– RICHARD FORTEY

"Bright reds –
scarlet, pillar-box red,
crimson or cherry
– are very cheerful
and youthful.
There is certainly
a red for everyone."

– CHRISTIAN DIOR

"*The best hiding spots
are not the most hidden;
they're merely the
least searched.*"

– CHRIS PAVONE

"I think penguins are the most human of all the birds, which may be why people love them. They're cute, they stand upright, and they look like they're wearing tuxedos."

– SHIA LABEOUF

Published in 2023 by Reed New Holland Publishers
Sydney

Level 1, 178 Fox Valley Road, Wahroonga, NSW 2076, Australia

newhollandpublishers.com

A record of this book is held at the National Library of Australia.

ISBN 9781921073496

Managing Director: Fiona Schultz
Publisher and Project Editor: Simon Papps
Designer: Andrew Davies
Production Director: Arlene Gippert
Printed in China

10 9 8 7 6 5 4 3 2 1

OTHER TITLES BY REED NEW HOLLAND INCLUDE:

Slater Field Guide to Australian Birds. Second Edition
Peter Slater, Pat Slater and Raoul Slater
ISBN 978 1 87706 963 5

Field Guide to Birds of North Queensland. Second Edition
Phil Gregory and Jun Matsui
ISBN 978 1 92554 625 5

Australian Birds In Pictures
Matthew Jones and Duade Paton
ISBN 978 1 92554 634 7

Parrot Conservation
Rosemary Low
ISBN 978 1 92554 646 0

Encounters With Australian Birds
Stephanie Jackson
ISBN 978 1 92554 695 8

A First Book of Beautiful Bird Songs (book with speaker)
Fred van Gessel
ISBN 978 1 92554 677 4

For details of these books and hundreds of other Natural History titles see

newhollandpublishers.com and follow ReedNewHolland on Facebook